OUT OF THE LAB
EXTREME JOBS IN SCIENCE

FORENSIC DETECTIVES

Katie Kawa

PowerKiDS
press.

New York

Published in 2016 by The Rosen Publishing Group, Inc.
29 East 21st Street, New York, NY 10010

First Edition

Editor: Katie Kawa
Designer: Mickey Harmon

Photo Credits: Cover Monty Rakusen/Cultura/Getty Images; p. 4 (inset) LukaTDB/Shutterstock.com; pp. 4–5 Edw/Shutterstock.com; pp. 6–7 Jon Bilous/Shutterstock.com; pp. 8–9, 17, 30 Couperfield/Shutterstock.com; p. 11 RTimages/Shutterstock.com; pp. 12–13 Jason Butcher/Cultura/Getty Images; p. 12 (inset) Jubal Harshaw/Shutterstock.com; pp. 14–15 (main) Peter Dazeley/Photographer's Choice/Getty Images; p. 15 (inset) Larysa Ray/Shutterstock.com; pp. 18–19 drohn/Shutterstock.com; p. 20 Fer Gregory/Shutterstock.com; p. 21 JOHAN ORDONEZ/Stringer/AFP/Getty Images; p. 23 UniversalImagesGroup/Contributor/Universal Images Group/Getty Images; pp. 24–25 Syda Productions/Shutterstock.com; p. 27 John B. Carnett/Contributor/Popular Science/Getty Images; pp. 28–29 Portland Press Herald/Contributor/Portland Press Herald/Getty Images.

Library of Congress Cataloging-in-Publication Data

Kawa, Katie, author.
 Forensic detectives / Katie Kawa.
    pages cm. — (Out of the lab: extreme jobs in science)
ISBN 978-1-5081-4521-9 (pbk.)
ISBN 978-1-5081-4522-6 (6 pack)
ISBN 978-1-5081-4523-3 (library binding)
1. Forensic sciences—Vocational guidance—Juvenile literature. 2. Forensic scientists—Juvenile literature. 3. Criminal investigation—Juvenile literature. I. Title.
 HV8073.8.K39 2016
 363.25—dc23
                           2015031620

Manufactured in the United States of America

CPSIA Compliance Information: Batch #BW16PK: For Further Information contact Rosen Publishing, New York, New York at 1-800-237-9932

Contents

BEHIND THE POLICE TAPE

Police officers put special tape around crime scenes to keep people away from these **dangerous** places. However, it's the job of some people to cross that tape and analyze, or study, the evidence left at a crime scene. These people are called forensic detectives.

Forensic detectives are sometimes called crime scene investigators, forensic investigators, or forensic scientists. They use science to analyze evidence and help the police find the person or people who committed a crime. These scientists often study blood, bullets, and other extreme pieces of evidence in order to catch deadly criminals.

Some forensic detectives study fires to find out who set them. Others study the effects of chemicals, such as deadly drugs, on a person's body. Thanks to the hard work of forensic detectives, science can help solve even the most mysterious crimes.

Forensic detectives are often hard at work behind the special tape meant to keep people away from dangerous, active crime scenes. It's their job to use science to figure out what happened at these crime scenes.

Forensic science is any kind of science used for legal purposes, such as solving crimes.

BRANCHES OF CRIME-SOLVING SCIENCE

There are many different kinds of forensic detectives and scientists. Some analyze the physical evidence at a crime scene, while others analyze the body of a person who was killed to find out more about how they died. Another group of forensic detectives is called to a crime scene when all that's found is bones.

All forensic detectives start in the same place—the classroom. Forensic detectives should have a strong background in science. They generally need to have a college degree in one of the natural sciences, such as chemistry or biology. It's also important for them to have taken math classes, because taking and comparing measurements and other kinds of **numerical data** is an important part of their job.

SCIENCE IN ACTION

Certain specialized forensic scientists need advanced degrees in one of the natural sciences. Some forensic scientists—especially scientists who study the bodies of murder victims—are medical doctors. They had to go to school for long time to become doctors.

These are just some of the branches of forensic science used to solve crimes. Each has its own educational requirements, but a degree in some kind of science is generally needed for any career in forensics.

Branches of Forensic Science

branch of forensic science	What does it study?	What kind of education does it call for?
criminalistics	physical evidence left at crime scenes	at least a four-year college degree in biology, chemistry, or forensic science
forensic anthropology	bones and other human remains left at a crime scene	a doctoral degree, which is the most advanced degree a person can get, in anthropology (the study of humans)
forensic pathology	physical harm done to a person's body, including the study of a dead body to find out the cause of death	a doctoral degree in medicine
forensic toxicology	the effects of drugs or other chemicals on the human body	at least a four-year college degree in a branch of natural science, especially chemistry
digital sciences	digital data, such as computer records and phone records, related to a crime	at least a four-year college degree in computer science, information technology, or engineering
odontology	dental remains left at a crime scene	a doctoral degree in dental surgery or dental medicine
forensic document examination	who wrote and signed pieces of writing	at least a four-year college degree in a field of science, especially forensic science

CRIMINALISTS AT A CRIME SCENE

General forensic detectives are also known as criminalists. They're the scientists who go to the crime scene and analyze the physical evidence found there. Sometimes, this analysis takes place at the crime scene itself, but it often takes place in a special laboratory called a crime lab.

Criminalists take photographs of the crime scene and the evidence they find there. They also take detailed notes about the location and position of evidence, including blood, hairs, and possible weapons found at the scene of a crime.

Because criminalists work at crime scenes, they have to be able to stay calm and clearheaded even when they see terrible things. Criminalists often see dead bodies, and they often have to look closely at blood and other unsettling pieces of evidence.

SCIENCE IN ACTION

Criminalists never stop learning! Throughout their career, they're trained in the latest methods of analyzing evidence. This allows them to be the best they can be at a job that often depends on the newest technology available to scientists.

A criminalist—like all forensic detectives—must be good at spotting details other people might miss. Sometimes the most important piece of evidence at a crime scene is the smallest.

CAREFULLY COLLECTING EVIDENCE

All forensic detectives have to be careful when handling evidence. If evidence is handled improperly, it can be considered tampered with or contaminated. Evidence tampering, or altering or destroying evidence, is a serious crime and can lead to time in jail. Contaminated evidence, or the introduction of something into a crime scene that wasn't there before, can sometimes cause a guilty person to go free or an innocent person to be put in jail.

To keep these things from happening, criminalists have to be especially careful with the evidence they get at crime scenes. They always wear gloves while handling evidence. They also put evidence into special bags or boxes using tools such as tweezers. Each piece of evidence collected must also be properly labeled.

SCIENCE IN ACTION

Forensic detectives must maintain the chain of custody with all pieces of evidence they collect. The chain of custody shows that evidence offered in court is the same as evidence collected at a crime scene. The chain of custody can be proven by keeping a record of every person who handles a piece of evidence.

Forensic detectives often deal with potentially harmful materials found at crime scenes. These include dangerous chemicals, weapons, and **bodily fluids** that could spread diseases. These scientists are trained to properly handle these materials in order to stay as safe as possible.

UNDER THE MICROSCOPE

What pieces of evidence do criminalists gather at crime scenes? They focus on physical evidence, which can range from the smallest strand of hair to objects as large as a car.

If a hair is found at a crime scene or on a victim's body, it can be compared to a suspect's hair under a microscope. The same can be done with fibers from clothing. Forensic detectives often study fibers found on a suspect to see if any match fibers from a victim's clothes. They can do the same with fibers found on a victim's body to see if they match fibers from a suspect's clothes.

Forensic scientists compare these samples in a lab using a tool called a comparison microscope. This kind of microscope allows them to see samples side by side under the same microscope.

FIBERS UNDER MICROSCOPE

SCIENCE IN ACTION

Hairs and fibers are common pieces of evidence because they can be easily transferred during physical contact.

After a forensic detective gathers a hair or fiber sample, they use a microscope to analyze it. Microscopes are important tools for all forensic scientists because they show details that can't be seen by human eyes alone.

OTHER KINDS OF EVIDENCE

Hairs and fibers aren't the only pieces of evidence forensic detectives analyze to help them solve a crime. They also study the bullets and **residue** left behind after a gun was fired at a crime scene. This type of analysis is called firearms identification.

Fingerprints were some of the first pieces of evidence ever studied at crime scenes. Fingerprint analysis involves collecting fingerprints from crime scenes using powder and lifting tape. Then, those fingerprints are compared with a set of known fingerprints, such as the fingerprints of a suspect. Forensic detectives can also study footprints left at a crime scene. They can compare the size of the shoe and the specific kind of shoe that left the print to shoes worn by a suspect.

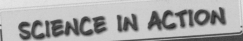

SCIENCE IN ACTION

The size, shape, and location of bloodstains at a crime scene can tell forensic detectives a lot about how a person was attacked, such as what kind of weapon was used and if the victim moved after they started bleeding. This kind of analysis is called bloodstain pattern analysis.

Forensic detectives know how to find a fingerprint match using the smallest details. Can you find the matching pair of fingerprints out of the examples shown here?

A NEW KIND OF FINGERPRINTING

While fingerprints, fibers, and bloodstains are all helpful in solving crimes, the most important piece of evidence a forensic detective can find at a crime scene is DNA. DNA is a substance in plant and animal cells that carries basic **genetic** information.

In 1984, a British scientist named Alec Jeffreys discovered a way to identify and compare different people's DNA. This process is known as DNA fingerprinting, and it's become a valuable method of analysis for forensic scientists.

Forensic scientists can find DNA in samples obtained from a crime scene, such as hairs and blood. They can even find DNA in skin cells found under a victim's fingernails. In that example, forensic scientists can compare the DNA found under the victim's fingernails to DNA from a suspect to see if they match.

SCIENCE IN ACTION

Everyone has different DNA, except for identical twins. However, scientists are working to come up with a method to find differences in the genetic material of identical twins. This could help forensic detectives tell the difference between their DNA if only one twin is a suspect in a criminal investigation.

Blood samples from crime scenes are good sources of DNA evidence. This kind of evidence has changed forensic science into a more exact science.

SOLVING COLD CASES WITH SCIENCE

DNA fingerprinting has proven to be very helpful for detectives looking to solve cold cases. A cold case is an unsolved case that can be reopened for investigation if new evidence is found. Often, that new evidence comes in the form of DNA. DNA fingerprinting has helped solve cold cases that are more than 50 years old!

DNA evidence discovered by forensic scientists has also been used by people working for The Innocence Project. The goal of The Innocence Project is to use DNA to **exonerate** people who've been imprisoned for crimes they didn't commit. As of 2015, over 300 people have been exonerated thanks to DNA fingerprinting. Also, over 150 of the real criminals in those cases have now been identified, thanks to the hard work of forensic detectives.

SCIENCE IN ACTION

When looking to solve very old cold cases using DNA evidence, forensic scientists often have to dig up the dead bodies of possible suspects and victims. That's the only way to get DNA samples from them.

Forensic scientists have helped solve many cold cases using the latest DNA fingerprinting technology.

STUDYING SKELETONS

When solving cold cases, special forensic scientists called forensic anthropologists are sometimes called in to help. A forensic anthropologist studies skeletons to find out how people died. Forensic anthropologists can find out if a person was shot, stabbed, or beaten by looking at what happened to their bones.

One forensic anthropologist has a television show based on her work! Kathy Reichs wrote books about her career as a forensic anthropologist. These books became the basis for a popular television show called *Bones*.

Reichs has used her skills as a forensic anthropologist to identify people killed in horrible attacks around the world. She went to New York City after the **terrorist** attacks of September 11, 2001, and worked to identify human remains found where the World Trade Center once stood.

SCIENCE IN ACTION

Bones can often reveal a person's gender, as well as their age and height when they died. This is very helpful when trying to identify victims using only their bones.

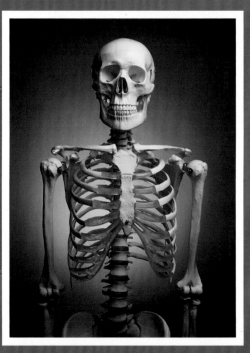

Skeletons may seem scary to some people. However, to forensic anthropologists, skeletons can hold the key to solving murder mysteries.

EXAMINING THE BODY

While forensic anthropologists study bones, another kind of forensic scientist studies the entire body of a murder victim to find out how they died. These scientists are called forensic pathologists, and—in some cases—they're also known as medical examiners.

Forensic pathologists look for bullet or stab wounds, bruises, or other marks on the body. Then, they study the body's organs. This is done through a kind of surgery called an autopsy. By studying the outside and inside of the body, forensic pathologists can discover what the victim was doing at their time of death.

Forensic pathologists sometimes work with other forensic scientists. They collect hairs and fibers on the body, as well as bodily fluids. These samples are then sent to criminalists as physical evidence.

SCIENCE IN ACTION

Sometimes it's hard for a forensic pathologist to determine a cause of death while looking at large parts of the body, such as whole organs. Instead, they often use a microscope to study small samples of **tissues** from a body.

Studying dead bodies might seem like a creepy career to some people, but forensic pathologists think it's a cool career—and an important one!

TESTING FOR DRUGS AND POISON

Forensic pathologists also work closely with forensic toxicologists. They often send samples of blood and other bodily fluids to forensic toxicologists for testing. It's the job of a forensic toxicologist to determine if drugs, alcohol, or poison was involved in a person's death.

Forensic toxicology is a branch of forensic science that calls for a very strong background in chemistry. These scientists use the most advanced technology available in hospitals, research labs, and crime labs to do their job.

Forensic toxicologists also test for drugs and alcohol in the bodies of people who are still alive. One example of this is in the world of sports. Forensic drug testing is done on athletes to test for the presence of performance-enhancing drugs in their body. Forensic toxicologists must analyze the samples given for these tests.

SCIENCE IN ACTION

All forensic scientists must be comfortable working with blood and other bodily fluids. Forensic toxicologists often test **urine** samples for the presence of drugs in a person's body.

Forensic toxicologists generally work in a lab, but the work they do in that lab is extreme. Not every scientist wants to analyze tubes of blood for traces of poison!

FORENSIC FIRE INVESTIGATION

A special kind of forensic detective analyzes fires, especially those believed to be set by arsonists, or people who purposely set fire to property. This kind of forensic detective is called a fire investigator.

Forensic fire investigation is a relatively new branch of forensic science. Leading the way in this field is the Bureau of Alcohol, Tobacco, Firearms and Explosives (ATF), which is a branch of the United States Department of Justice.

The ATF's Fire Research Laboratory, which was built in 2003, is unlike any other lab in the world. Engineers built it to study what causes certain fires and how fires spread. To study these things, this building houses a burn room. There, buildings can be constructed and set on fire inside the lab!

SCIENCE IN ACTION

The engineers that designed the ATF's Fire Research Laboratory wanted to make it as safe for the **environment** as possible. They even created a system that collects and recycles the water used to put out test fires.

Fire investigators use science to help them determine the cause of a fire. To do this, they have to visit the scene of a fire, which can be very dangerous.

COMPUTERS AND CRIME

Forensic science is a field that's constantly changing. As computers began playing a larger role in criminal activity, an entire new branch of forensic science emerged. It's called digital sciences, or computer forensic science.

Detectives who specialize in computer forensic science work to find, preserve, and present data found on computers and other digital devices—including smartphones—that could be useful in solving a crime. They look for the people a suspect or victim communicated with through email or social media. They look for online banking records or other records of money spent, including money spent on travel.

Computer forensic scientists also have the means of recovering deleted information. This is very helpful when analyzing a suspect's computer for data that might prove the suspect committed a crime.

SCIENCE IN ACTION

Forensic detectives who specialize in digital science might also analyze other forms of technology used by criminals. These include voice-changing devices and computer programs used to hide their identity. Certain forensic detectives have skills that allow them to discover the person's real voice and appearance.

If you like computers and want to solve crimes, then you might want to consider a career in forensic computer science. These forensic detectives often go to school for computer science.

A FUTURE IN FORENSICS

No matter what area of forensics a scientist specializes in, they need to be prepared to deal with extreme situations. They analyze bloody crime scenes, see the aftermath of terrible fires, dig up human bones, and study dead bodies. If you want to be a forensic detective or any kind of forensic scientist, you need to be able to stay calm and think clearly in situations that might scare other people.

Forensic detectives know science is often the key to solving a crime. If a future in forensics sounds fun to you, science and math classes are the place to start. Those classes will give you the tools you need to have an exciting career solving crimes with science!

GLOSSARY

bodily fluid: A liquid that comes from inside a person's body.

dangerous: Not safe.

environment: The natural world around us.

exonerate: To prove that someone is not guilty of a crime.

genetic: Referring to the parts of cells that control the appearance, growth, and other traits of a living thing.

numerical data: Facts or other pieces of information presented as numbers that can be used in different ways.

residue: A small amount of something that remains after a process has been completed.

terrorist: A person who uses violence to scare people as a way of achieving a political goal.

tissue: A group of cells of the same kind that come together to form the basic parts that make up a plant or animal.

urine: Liquid waste from a person or animal's body.

INDEX

WEBSITES

Due to the changing nature of Internet links, PowerKids Press has developed an online list of websites related to the subject of this book. This site is updated regularly. Please use this link to access the list:
www.powerkidslinks.com/exsci/fdet